As Things Come

Enid Dorrett J-Ellis

PublishAmerica
Baltimore

© 2008 by Enid Dorrett J-Ellis.
All rights reserved. No part of this book may be reproduced, stored in a retrieval system or transmitted in any form or by any means without the prior written permission of the publishers, except by a reviewer who may quote brief passages in a review to be printed in a newspaper, magazine or journal.

First printing

PublishAmerica has allowed this work to remain exactly as the author intended, verbatim, without editorial input.

ISBN: 1-60563-405-0
PUBLISHED BY PUBLISHAMERICA, LLLP
www.publishamerica.com
Baltimore

Printed in the United States of America

This book is dedicated to the people in my life that I love and hold dear in my heart that were and still continue to be there to help me with situations in life "as they come".

Jessie Mae Greene Jenkins (Momma)

Jefffery Jenkins, Jr. (Poppa)

John Steven Kevern (My Buddha)

512th Memorial Affairs Squadron
&
The Port Mortuary
(My Family)

As Things Come

To ~~Kirstin~~ Karen,

Hey girl, Karen,
I hope you enjoy the readings and find therapy in them for yourself & others...
I hope we continue getting to know one another.

"Emil"

The Betrayal

She trusted you
With life and love.

She trusted you and
When thing got worse
She became a curse,
Casted away like bait
On a reel
While you go out
Adopting the lifestyle of a heel

She trusted you to be there
But you didn't care.
You left her to go, where?
To your second home to roam
And continue your game of lust.

Point of No Return

Where did you go?

We loved you
And what did you do?
You left and abandoned us
Turning a family of three into two.
You're no where in sight
For the purpose of wording
A fight and
Your marriage has lost its might.
For better or worse
You were to be there,
Instead you're invisible
And act as if you don't care.

Where did you go?

Its mom and me
Can't you see?
You've caused nothing but misery.
I hope you're happy
With what you've done
And as far as love
There is none.
It disappeared as you did
The jar now has a lid.
This chapter is closed
You hid from the lives
You could have saved,
But no instead you caved.

Where did you go?

DADDY!!!!!!

Gone

You don't have a house
You don't have a wife
You don't have a child
You don't have a family
You don't have a life
You don't have a personality
You don't have a mind
You don't have a conscious
You don't have integrity
You don't have friends
You don't have good times
You don't share the laughter
You don't cry the tears
You don't see the loneliness
You don't feel abandoned
You don't have the heartache
You don't have the support
You don't care
You don't carry the scars
You don't have the memories
You don't have anything anymore
You don't have love
You don't have a clue, do you?

My Momma

Who taught me how to pray at night
Tucked me into bed real tight
So I could dream of stars so bright?

My Momma.

Who walked with me till I walked alone
Listen to my moans and groans
Taught me to talk in a special tone?

My Momma.

Who did things for me until it was done myself
Called me her little, little elf
Put each picture of me on the shelf?

My Momma.

Who took care of me when I was ill
Always paid the phone bill
Always told me to keep still?

My Momma.

Who taught me things I had to learn
In each activity gave me a turn
Gave me rewards that I had to earn?

My Momma.

All around from coast to coast
You will always hear me boast
About the person I love most.

My Momma.

This poem is dedicated to the memory of My Mother

Jessie Mae Greene Jenkins

Sunrise: March 11, 1946—Sunset: February 22, 2005

Coping

You left today
In a quiet way
But not in vain.

As each day passes
I grow stronger
In coping with the pain,
Of losing someone
Who meant so much.
My heart is the one
That's touched.
By your memory of
What and how much you've
Meant to me.

This poem is dedicated to the memory of My Mother

Jessie Mae Greene Jenkins

Sunrise: March 11, 1946—Sunset: February 22, 2005

Where to Go?

I walk alone,
Not knowing what road I'm on.

Or in what direction
To complete the connection.

What path to travel
When life starts to unravel.

Or uncharted waters to sail
In search of self
In order to prevail.

An unknown course awaits my plotting
From the norm,
I soon will be departing.

While a map unread holds the secret of where to tread,
On a road from which so many have fled.

To seek the revelation, discovery,
And control of my own destiny.

Tested

Where am I
Lost
Tossed
Out of every
Open window
Pane
No aim
No trust
Turned to rust
Blown away like dust
Ashes
Flashes of betrayal
All alone
Prone
To forces unknown
From all walks of life
Strife
Comes at me
When I least can see
Why me?
See
In this predicament
I never asked to be
Involved
Problem solved
By a solution
Resolution.
Needs to take place
Remove from my face
The mask of stress
More becoming less

Is this a test?
Pass or fail
I will prevail.

Questions?

Have you ever been
Where I've been
Feeling like you've
Been done in
With no one upon
Which to depend
Lost inside
Yourself, where you
Continue to hide
Silencing your voice
Because you feel
You have no choice
But to go on
Experiencing the torment
Of thoughts
Unpleasant; unknown
Piercing
Your mind's eye
Feelings invading
And waiting from
Which you cannot defend
And gain freedom
From a troubled world
Into which we're hurled
To discover peace
Where the noise has ceased
Combing the earth
In search of rebirth
Evaluating your own self-worth.

Answers!

You have to go on
Stand strong
No matter what
May be going wrong
And right in life
Face the strife
Truth sometimes cuts like a knife
Time heals all and many a wound
And very soon
A new tune will arise
From all the gloom
And all will become new
Life will return to normal soon
Out goes fear
In come confidence
Your outlook positive
In every sense
You're scared
But be prepared
To live the future
That once by all
Was dared
As windows and doors
Begin to open
The sunlight of dreams and possibilities
Shine rays of hope in
Ready to enter the world
Refreshed, refocused, and renewed
With no thought of how you're viewed
Is how you'll navigate from now on
A new destiny is what you will create.

The Path

From the years to come
I know where I am from.

A course has been planned
And by God it is manned.

The breath of life installed
With a purpose,
For which I have been called.

I must be me
In order to be set free
And fulfill my divine destiny.

Whether it be alone
Or with someone
The task…at hand
Must and will be done.

The Course

As each day passes
With fleeting force,
I constantly wonder
About the single purpose destined
For me among the masses.

Happiness, Sadness
Success or failure,
The trials and tribulations
In store for me, myself
To endure.

Even though time grows short,
I am armed with the knowledge
There is a chosen path
I cannot abort.
For it belongs to me
In order to be free.

With God by my side,
My hand in his,
Facing fears from which I cannot hide.
Faith is my sword and shield
To encounter challenges
As they come and not yield.

In the Mirror

Where are you? / In search of me.
Here I am/ Where did you begin?
Can't you see me? / I'm right here.
Where am I? / I don't know.
Search me.

Elements of Life

LOVE
Is given with the purest of hearts
JOY
Is given with the sound of laughter
HAPPINESS
Is given with a smile on one's face
SACRIFICE
Is given without thought of one's self
KINDNESS
Is given without a price
DEVOTION
Is given when earned with time
RESPECT
Is given with reverence from others
HONESTY
Is found where lies cannot enter
PEACE
Comes when all worries are gone

Can't Change Me

You think you know what you see
But you don't know me,
Just observing me physically.

Don't judge a book by its cover
The days of assumption are over.

To wonder who I am and what makes me tick,
If all rumors will stick.

Instead of knowing me by yourself
I am immediately placed on your shelf.

To collect dust gathered by you and others
While you and the rest wallow in your druthers.

I go on being me, absolutely free
While watching you and others just the same
Drown in self pity.

What others think no longer embrace my mind
Only positive words and people are what I seek to find.

Just Don't, OK?

Don't complain.
It is the negative
From which you will refrain.

Don't wine; there is no time,
For there are positives
Of which you will find.

Don't cry; press on
And search until
You find your why.

Don't frown; turn it upside down
For a smile
Can stretch happiness, mile for mile.

Don't look down.
Aim your eyes upward
For the inspiration
To move forward.

Don't tarry and
Wonder off your path.
Clouds always clear
In the aftermath.

Don't worry,
Settle down and take your time
To see what lies ahead
Instead of rushing through life in a hurry.

Regrouping

Time heals all wounds.
The ugly of the past is
Now entombed.

Forgiveness sets in,
Bringing the cancer of negativity
To an end.

There are things I could
Have done differently
That now seem
To come to me.

Flashbacks of scenes
In my dreams,
Of handling situations
By other means.

It seems only right
To view all things as good;
See the other side as bright.

No longer will the world seem dim
As long as I look up to the sky
To seek and speak to him.

Released

I am happy to be me.
I'm free
To see
The life that is
To be
And planned divinely.

I am happy to be me.
I'm free
To sing out loud
To the world
I'm proud
No longer living behind
A negative shroud.

I am happy to be me.
I'm free
To discover new things
Spread my wings
And experience what each day brings.

I am happy to be me.
I'm free
To conquer my fears
Be open to express the feelings
That have been bottled up for so many years.

I am happy to be me.
I'm free
To know that I did not depend on man
To get me where I am
But on God
Who continues to hold my hand.

Untitled

The world of today
Is not the world of yesterday.
Nor will it be tomorrow.
There is too much sorrow
An abstinence of happiness
Lurks throughout the atmosphere
And ongoing mayhem is prevalent
And persists in this human existence.

The lack of peace in the lives
Of mankind is a dictator
Owning many minds
And brings destruction to family lines.

In mayday mode we stand
Seeking consistency in our reality
As the pendulum of time
Continues to swing
And time gradually ticks away all hope of resolution
To the foundations of once civil institutions.
Built with pride and patriotism
Which now operate in sheer confusion.

A Sea of Trouble

Follow me...
Follow me...
Follow me...
Into the
Deep
Deep
Sea of:

Blue—depression, sadness, worry, loneliness, despair, sorrow

Yellow—sickness, tragedy, fear, desertion, abandonment

Green—envy, jealousy, perverseness, power, greed

Red—fury, anger, rage, infatuation, vengeance, hate, strength, dominance, passion, corruption

Black—solitude, isolation, blindness, pain, death, evil, confusion

Into the whirlpool we go
Deeper and
Deeper and
Deeper
Into a fate
We don't know,
Has in store for us.

The world is an ocean of turmoil
Ebbing and
Flowing with chaos.

Untitled

Those who are open, to truly care
A concept this world of today cannot bare.

Too much fear and doubt
Is what they shout,
Good versus evil, a constant bout.

Setting the tone
To face alone, the aim to claim
Our identities and spirits as our own.

Those who risk their lives
For others to survive
In this conflicting world
Living in constant turmoil
Into what seems infinity, indefinitely?

Too busy to share
The secrets we keep
So we can remain discreet
In hopes that no ones true selves will be made aware.

A Link

A complete stranger you walked in,
Unaware that between you and I,
A strong bond would begin.
There you were unknown to me,
A key,
To my life you soon would be
To unlock the doors of
The darkness of my past
And build new memories
Sure to last.

As time passes, together, we
Continue to grow
Not knowing or worrying of
Which direction it will go.
You stuck by me
And I you.

Devotion to one another
Shines through
To others that watch and
Constantly ponder about
Our connection to each other.

It's not for them to understand
What god had planned.
All that matters is that
We do,
Just us two,
In hopes it will continue.

Forever in each other's
Life and heart to stay.
We like it that way.
You from me and
Me from you
We'll never stray.

Ode to "John"

In the two years that have passed
Getting to know one another
Has been a blast.

Knowing you
Is one of the best experiences
To go through.

You've brighten my days
In so many ways.

Ups and downs
Smiles and frowns
Trust in you
Is what I've found.

Promise me before you go
Our solid bond will
Continue to grow.

Staying in touch
Cause I miss you
So much.

Thinking of you fondly
While you're away
With each passing day.

With tears of sorrow
And the passing of each
Today, yesterday, and tomorrow.

Awaiting your return, while
Postponing our times of
Joy and abundant laughter
Till we meet again
The year after.

Then you'll have to come back
Before you know and we'll
Ask "Where did the time go?"

(Dedicated to my best friend "John Steven Kevern"
before leaving for Korea = "I Love You"!!!)

Friendships Are Forever (2 Poems)

It's a nice to know what
Friends are for.
They come in a kinds
Rich and poor.
Telling secrets behind
A closed door.
Wondering what the
Future has in store.

Maybe together,
Maybe apart.
With knowledge of one another,
As a memory,
In their heart.

Parting Words to the IRHS Class of 1988

Old, new, special
And true
The best that life
Has to offer
There is where they've
Always been
Through the good and bad,
Thick and thin
You are what you are
The greatest treasure
By far

You mean the world
To me too
I love and will miss
Each and every one of you.

Day Dreamer

Off into another world or your own.
Taking time to be alone,
In a zone,
Your mind sets the tone as smaller ideas
Have grown,
Into bigger dreams
That were sown
Into realistic
Ventures unknown

Inspiration

Oh how wonderful you are
My bright and shining star.

Lighting the optimism of
My future, in dreams
Of which you constantly nurture.

Ideas flowing like a waterfall
In a lifetime fit it all.

Imagination running wild
Like that of a naïve child.

Creativity is abound
With thoughts old and new
That are found.

Untitled

You are the fulfillment of my needs
Whether it be in words or deeds.
The igniter of my fires
Which yearn,
Causing my heart to burn
With sweet desires
You are the fill in the blank
It's you I thank.
You are the backbone
So I am never prone
To fight any battle alone.

Spiritual Inquiry

I want to know
Where you live:
"In your heart and spirit
Is where I dwell
And all is well."

I want to know
Your voice:
"Just be silent and still
You will."

I want to know
When to hold your hand:
"Reach up in praise joyfully
And I'll hold on eternally."

I want to know
When you are near:
"Where two or three are gathered in my name
I'm here."

I want to know
Where you are:
"Look up into the night sky
For the brightest star shining high."

I want to know
How you love:
"I watch over and guard
My children from the
Heavens above."

I want to know
My service to you:
"Love your brothers, sisters,
And me as I do you."

Watchful Shepherd

You are there
In troubled time
And moments sublime.

You are there
Inspiring me to press on
Because the day is not gone.

You are there
Helping to battle my fears
The little voice inside my ears.

You are there
Offering guidance and love
From the heavens above.

You are there
No matter what the storm
To restore our faith
To return to the norm.

You are there
Through each sunrise and sunset
Securing that the desires
Of our hearts are met.

You are there
In our journey of life
Whether it be during
Peace or strife.

You are there
You are everywhere
And that is how
We know you care.

C-A-N Y-O-U

Can you hear me
        Saying it
                Yelling it
            Screaming it
                Shouting it
            Whispering it
              Singing it
                  Telling it
                Talking about it

Can you see me
            Writing it
        Excited about it
        Happy about it
        Prancing about it
        Overjoyed about it
                Smiling about it
  Jumping up and down about it

Can you tell it by the touch?
Can you feel it in the air?

I L-O-V-E Y-O-U !!!!!!!!

Happy Thought

My love is stored
In a special place
Just for you,
Only to be revealed
In times of joy and
Especially when you're blue.

It fills my heart
Rejuvenating my spirit
With intense passion,
Surging throughout my core
Whether you're near
Or far apart.

It rattles my bones
In knowing your touch
Will just send me
To places unknown,
In my mind
Awakening once dormant hormones.

It makes me swoon
Anticipating the time
When we'll share,
In the moments of
Each day and night together soon.

My Fantas-He

He moves like the spirit of the wind
The bobbing of the waves on the ocean's surface
The galloping motion of a horse's hooves
Is the thumping of my rapid heart
When he is close to me

Free, free, flowing like a summer breeze
His stares sweep me off into
Another dimension of dreams
In such a fashion
That sometimes it's love and also passion.

Warm and tender are his eyes
Whether they be of placid hazel lakes, ocean blue pools,
Or sweet ginger brown
As they beam, sparkle, and shine
Rays of happiness and hope into mine.

Deeper into the Soul of He

I'll tell you what I see in the man.
In his eyes I see
A most precious light
That's never lost;
But where his wonderful spirit
Is found
And I know this by the way he smiles.

I'll tell you what I feel from the man.
Its power like no other;
Of so much love;
Of so much passion;
And I know this by the way he talks.

I'll tell you what I think of the man.
With earnest ear I hear his words;
So many hopes;
So many dreams;
So many ambitions;
And I know this by the way he lives.

No Rush

One day at a time
Just you and me,
Not knowing what the
Future will be.

Taking it slow
As we go,
For what?
We'll never know.

Just you and I
As the days go by,
Years have passed
One after another,
And still we are
In love with
Each other.

It's great because
With each year,
We still have things
To share.
And know that two
People, you and me, are
Around to care and
For one another be there.

Picture of Us

I believe in we
Together a force so strong
A solid foundation even
When things go wrong.
We hear the sound of our
Own song of love
A lifetime long.

The spiritual bond we
Display is our essence
To those who are
In our presence,
And pass our way
Tomorrow, yesterday, and today.

Never appearing as or
Feeling like strangers
But close friends,
Partners and lovers.

There are many who wish
To be in our places,
While witnessing far away or up close
The shared laughter and smiles
On our faces.

Our mutual attention
Communicates sincerity
Without our mention.
The devotion is evident
Without need to question.

Pleasant Uncertainty

Press your lips against mine.
Forget all sense of time and
Let our souls intertwine.

Watch inhibitions leave.
Gone without reprieve increasing
The intensity we weave.
Matched by our arms
Around each other
No outside thoughts
To interfere or bother.

Sharing in the moment
It's ours and we own it.

Our hearts on fire
With sheer passion and desire.

No reservations
Just accepting the sensations
Leading up to our sensual destination.

Where we'll arrive
We don't know.

Our intense adventure
Is in front of us.
It's in each other
We'll have to trust.

1 Night Stand

Two hearts
Burning
Yearning
Soon unite
For a time
They know is right.

Be strong
Hold on
To the feelings
Inside.
Desire has taken over
There's nothing to hide.

All dreams, hopes, fears
And pride
Have been
Set aside
To enjoy our sultry ride.

Told Ya So

I told ya so
It be us two.
Here together
Me and you.

I told ya so
I'd never let go.
I have your love
And I want mo.

I told ya so
Our love would grow.
Overstepping boundaries
No one would go.

I told ya so
Your joy and pain.
Is with me
Just the same.

I told ya so
Our feelings are true.
Always together
Me and you.

I told ya so
We'll never part.
You'll always
Live within
My heart.

Untitled Love

Stay with me always,
With the promise that neither of us strays
Or falls prey,
To the temptation of another.

Pledge your love,
Even when push comes to shove,
All of the above
Close to one another's heart.

Display your affection
As a confirmation of our connection,
And an eternal affirmation
That we are united as one.

Abide by me,
As we
Happily
Travel this sojourn together

Embrace our adventures,
Sharing in the times and treasures,
In all of life's measures
Then, now, and always forever and ever.

Inevitable

Stay with me, Let it be
And see
Whether you and me
Can be.

If love will blossom
And become something awesome
No longer feeling lonesome
Having dreamt of this moment to come.

Our feelings are mutual
Not pretend, but actual
Beyond theory; absolutely factual
The idea of mystery becoming certainty wonderful.

A chance to explore
And find out more
Of what's in store
Behind this once closed, but now opened door.

Moment of Truth

Come close; be near
Listen and hear
To what I'll whisper
In your ear.
A secret long carried and can no longer bear
Of thoughts loving and sincere
To the one I hold so dear.
And yet so mere
It's crystal clear
The feelings on my sleeve I wear
May be in danger.
As I fear
The moment you stare
Into my eyes and peer
And realize how much I care
While I await your answer in despair
That these same emotions you share.

Giving, Loving, and Devoting

I'm so glad
My mind lets me think of you
Bringing your smile into constant view.

I'm so glad
My eyes light up and overflow with tears
As I reflect on the good years.

I'm so glad
My body can be contained in your arms
And fall innocently into your charms.

I'm so glad
My hands fit yours to guide me through for
What life has in store.

I'm so glad
My ears can hear the sweet nothings whispered by your voice
That loving you more and more is the only choice.

The Chance I've Dreamed Of

From daybreak to sunset
Of many years gone by,
My lonesome heart has
Watched the tears I cry;
As I wished that some day
My chance would come
To give my precious love away.

But not to just anyone
Who happens to come my way,
Just to that one person
For in God's name I pray.
Someone to hold.
Someone to care.
Someone to love.
Will I ever find the one
I'm thinking of?

And when I wasn't looking
You soon appeared;
When I least expected it,
At last you're here.

Through all the loneliness
And all the broken hearts,
I've finally found you,
And from you I'll never part.

Its destiny that brought us
Together, not coincidence.
There's just something
About us that makes sense.

So now that you're here
I hope you'll decide to stay,
And face the trials and tribulations
We'll encounter, come what may.

You heard my cry
And answered my call.
You came and were there
To break my fall.

The one I needed, wanted,
With which to share my love;
And now you are here;
The chance I've dreamed of.

Harmonial Surprise

A kiss I dreamed
Lasting forever it seemed
While in the arms of someone,
Holding me tight
Basking in the warmth of sunlight.

My mind
Penetrating with bliss
With each impending kiss,
A mystery, the face
On which each kiss is placed.

The unknown accepted
Although the vision unexpected
Enjoyed and respected,
While the features
Of this person go undetected.

And yet I feel no danger
As this passionate exchange
Occurs between my lips
And the lips of this unknown stranger,
My mind is contemplating, debating
Whether to bring him into focus
Or continue this pleasurable cliffhanger.

I'll await his identity
As this moment goes on
To be revealed in reality,
What could be a sign of
Pending true love destined for me.

It's Ours

The love we make
It's ours.
The good times we have
It's ours.
The laughter we share
It's ours.
The moments we kiss
It's ours.
The times we're together
It's ours.
The obstacles we overcome
It's ours.

Every second,
Minute,
Hour,
Day,
Week,
Month,
And year
It's ours.

The joys and sorrows
It's ours.
What we have
It's all ours.

Gaining Meaning

I value the times spent in your arms
Enveloped by your adoring charms
That set off my physical
As well as mental alarms
Causing a multitude of pleasant
Thoughts to gather and swarms
In my mind and the best
Of my heart warms
Up my love while
The anxiety in my spirit calms
The once crippling fears and
Drying the all too many flowing tears
That plagued the inner me.

I accept, while with you, the peace that comes
Which in total sums
Up and destroys the pain
That no longer numbs
Because joy and happiness have set in
And gladly my will succumbs
To your devotion and affection
As the rhythm of my heart hums
To the sound of yours
Accompanied by emotional outpours
Affirming our solid union.

I appreciate the care you take
And every effort you make
To guard my soul
So that my heart will no longer ache
From scornful feelings of my past
To protect the bond we share

Not only for yours, but our sake
Because being with you is my reward
As we move forward
In our journey of life together.

The Storm Before the Calm

Twisting
Writhing
Breathing
Panting
Gliding
Pressing
Pleasure
Euphoric
Griping

Stroking
Groping
Feeling
Touching
Gasping
Screaming
Climaxing

Intense
Building
Exotic
Immense
Emotional
Weakening
Strengthening
Physical

Easing
Soothing
Relieving
Relaxing

Teasing
Pleasing
Satisfying
Gratifying
Wet
Wild
Passionate
Romantic
Togetherness
Honest

Calming
Peaceful
Stillness
Fulfilling

Oneness
Wholeness

Expression of Mine Own Love for Thee

My love is with thee
All day. All night.
At the break of morning light.

While my love is with thee
I have no reason for fright
And I know that you, I, and
Everything is just right.

My love is with thee
Through the quietest of storm,
When I am without you
My aching heart mourns.

When my love is with thee
I feel reborn
Not sensing the pain,
Depression, sorrow, and
Heartache of a woman scorned.

My love is with thee
In all my sweetest of dreams,
Caring about, sharing with,
And holding one another—
The most gentle, and tender of scenes.

My love is with thee
In the Future,
In the Present,'
In the Past
Always and forever to
Last and last and last.

Everywhere my love is
With thee and I too,
Hope that thine's
Love is with me.

Nothing's Changed

We were in love then
And we're still in love now

Together
Apart
In laughter
And joy
In sadness
Good times
Bad times
Trials
Tribulations
Full of passion
And desire

No matter
What life
Hands us

We're still in love now
As we were then.

Ultimate Devotion

We met
At heaven's bet
You and me
Became we
Now united
Divinely invited
Into each other's lives
All tests survived
As we kiss
Days of loneliness
Away to the past
We will last
Through sands of time
Our souls intertwine
With sunlight and sunset
From at first glance
We met.

Attraction

Meeting for the first time
Already accepting you as mine
As my heart sighs
While you're held in my eyes
My emotions dance
As I'm caught in this trance
Not a word from my lips
My mind slips
Into loving daydreams
Of you and I it seems
As a happy pair
A vision so clear
That I know and see
With you is where I want to be.

Hear Me Out...

You really don't understand
How much you mean to me.
It was the powers that be
Heaven sent
Is how we met.

You really don't understand
The dark clouds you've
Sent away,
So I could wake up and
Smile each and every day.

You really don't understand
How your light shines,
And warms my life
When I feel oncoming strife.

You really don't understand
That I am with you
Where ever you go,
It's evident in the love
Towards you I show and
With each passing year our
Bond seems to grow.

But I understand you,
The person you are.
I know you'll always be with me
No matter how near or far.

Until Your Return

I miss you
A hug and kiss are due.

I miss you
Every moment together
Makes me feel new.

I miss you
We as a couple
The perfect view.

I miss you
All day and night through.

I miss you
With a longing heart
Until you're in sight I'm blue.

I miss you
Thoughts of the two of us
Stick in my mind like glue.

I miss you
When you're gone and come back
I know exactly what to do.

I miss you
But my love is strong
Moments of weakness are few.

I miss you
Distance is a stranger
Closeness is what grew.

I miss you
Quality; not quantity
Is the clue.

I miss you
There is no one
Else to pursue.

I miss you
The bond we share
Is true.

I miss you
And I know
You miss me too.

L.O.V.E.

I love you.
What more can I do
It's true.

I love you.
What more can I say
Each time you pass my way.

I love you.
What more can I feel
This is real.

I love you.
What more can I hear
Than the sound of my heartbeat
Whenever you are near.

I love you.
What more can I taste
But the sweetness of your kisses
Without haste.

I love you.
What more can I touch
But the face of the one
I adore so much.

I love you.
What more can I see
But the smile on your face
As you stare back at me.

Loving Moment

My fingers to your lips I trace
While envisioning your smiling face.

Memories o' so sweet rush in
As your hand gently caresses my skin.

Tenderly and lovingly in each other's eyes we stare
Silently expressing how much we care.

We hold another tight
Causing our spirits to unite in delight.

As we lean in
For the moment when our lips will blend.

Into a sweet never ending kiss
Fulfilling our long time wish.

To share our lives in good and bad times
All of the above, always forever in love.

Waiting for You

I'm waiting for you to take my hand
And walk on the beach in the warm sand.

I'm waiting for you to bring me joy
The kind no one can destroy.

I'm waiting for you to enter my soul
To reveal hidden feelings and
Make them unfold.

I'm waiting for you to embrace my fears
Calm my worries and dry my tears.

I'm waiting for you to mend my heart
For in the past it was once torn apart.

I'm waiting for you to whisper my name
So it makes me feel richer
Than fortune and fame.

I'm waiting for you to accept me as I am
Voluntarily; not by force or command.

I'm waiting for you and this is true
Because I have so much love for you.

The Knight in American Armor

Broad and strong, he stands there tall
Surveying the land
In a stolid stance.
Ready, alert
At attention
Prepared to defend
When his countrymen call.

A gallant warrior
Of red, white, and blue.
Fighting for his nation,
His country,
And all that is true.

Eternal father strong to save
This soldier of sea, land, or air.
Who's mighty, fierce
And oh so brave;

In the name of freedom
So the flag may wave
In constant glory
Showing the world
It knows victory.

*(This poem is dedicated to the service men
and women defending our country in times of war)*

Equality

What is the difference between you and I?

So many of them against us
Why?
Why?

You, me,
We are one and the same.

Human beings
Who want to be free
To love and treat
Each other equally.

Not by race, creed, color, or religion,
But as persons
In hopes to make the world
A better place: a more than worthy common vision.

A King's Dream

"I have a dream", a king once said;
To have peace, love, and harmony
Fill every colorful head."

He spoke of togetherness
Across the Motherland
In hopes that we, one day,
As a country will work with one another
Hand in hand.

His life was the price
He did pay
In trying to show the world
A better way
To live as one, without discrimination,
In hopes that eyes of the future
Will be proud of their nation.

(This poem is dedicated to the late great Reverend Dr. Martin Luther King, Jr.)

The Walk of Ruby Bridges

I WANT:

To laugh, dance, play, and sing.
To be able to do most anything.
To do my best in what I'm in
And not be judged by the color of my skin.
To have those see me for what I am
On the outside and in.

I am filled with so much
Pride to know who I am.
To be aware that my roots are firm
As well as my faith.
In God I trust
Not prejudice and hate.

A child then and a woman now
Who knows no bounds.
Battling ignorance without
One sound.

I walk; in silence
Towards the school doors
On this crowded, noisy block.

If I Were a Turkey

If I were a turkey
I'd set me a trap;
I'd hide in the woods,
And make me a map

I'd draw out a plan to
Trick the human race;
It would be good
It would lead to disgrace.

My turkey friends and I
We'd play a game;
When man came to hunt us
We'd make them ashamed.

We'd get us some rope
And hide in hope;
That when they came a lookin for us
We'd tie them by the knees
And hang em up in the trees.

We'd tie them up in knots
And leave them in the woods;
Then we would put on our
Man's suits and hoods

We'd strut to their houses
And turn our selves in
We'd look at their wives
And flash them a grin

We'd say "Here we are ladies
Ready to be cooked!"
Can you imagine their faces?
As we stood in our places.

They will probably turn and run
And that will be our fun.

HAPPY THANKSGIVING DAY!!!! : From the Turkey

Christmas Thoughts

Christmas is a time of year
That brings laughter and good cheer.
Silver bells are what we hear
Ringing through the atmosphere.

We celebrate with loved ones and friends
And do our yearly Christmas trends.
We like it so much that we cannot comprehend
Why this holiday, each year, has to end.

We carol with glee
As we trim the tree
Ever oh so beautifully.
Christmas means so much to me
That I feel like I'm in luxury.

Sugarplums and candy canes
Snowflakes on the window panes
Are visions that we think of.
The snow on the ground looks
White and soft and soft like the feathers
Of a turtle dove.

The aroma of cookies fills the air
That you cannot wait to taste them in despair.
You can tell that Grandma baked each cookie
With tender, loving care.

A warm blazing fire
Shines like a lantern.
As we wrap our gifts with
Paper of a pretty pattern.

Time to rest now, all is done.
Up the stairs we all so run
And climb into bed,
Until morning when we see the sun.

Then we jump right up
And gallop down the steps
Without a fuss,
To see what Old Saint Nicholas
Left for us.

Christmas is a time of joy
That brings excitement
To a girl and boy.
So always remember and never fret,
Christmas is a holiday noone ever
Wants to forget.

Hot Chocolate!!!

Nice and sweet, so hot
It warms your feet
Tickling your taste buds, toes,
And tummy Oooh Hot Chocolate
Mmmmmmm yummy yummy!!!
Poor me a cup
Of that scrumptious Joe
Not too much, that's
Enough Woah!! Woah!!
Filling is with marshmallows
Turns it into a melted smore.

After the first cup
Please pour me more.
Now I'll face the winter air,
Without a care,
Without a thought.
Because of that Hot Chocolate I drank
From this morning's coffee pot.

The 4 Seasons

Spring is beautiful.
Summer is hot.
Fall is in between and
Winter is not.

In the Spring the flowers
Begin to bloom
And everything is ready
In June.

Summer brings the
Hot, hot sun,
But this is when
We have our fun.

In the Fall of the year,
The leaves begin to change colors.
It's like a picture
Worth a million dollars.

Winter brings the snow
That covers the land.
It's white and pretty,
And feels good in your hand.

This is my rhyme.
This is my reason.
I hope you too enjoy
The four seasons.

Imparting Words

"Life is a journey and affords many experiences, good and bad. Each experience makes us stronger. Life has no order. It just happens and it up to us to handle, to the best of our abilities with what God gives us, situations in life "as things come".